First published in hardback in Great Britain in 2011 by Orion Books an imprint of the Orion Publishing Group Ltd Orion House, 5 Upper St Martin's Lane, London WC2H 9EA
An Hachette UK Company

10 9 8 7 6 5 4 3 2 1

A CIP catalogue record for this book is available from the British Library.

ISBN: 978 1 409 13250 9

Design & Illustration OBRoberts
Editorial Jane Sturrock

Printed and bound in Spain

The Orion Publishing Group's policy is to use papers that are natural, renewable and recyclable and made from wood grown in sustainable forests. The logging and manufacturing processes are expected to conform to the environmental regulations of the country of origin.

Every effort has been made to fulfil requirements with regard to reproducing copyright material. The author and the publisher will be glad to rectify any omissions at the earliest opportunity.

www.orionbooks.co.uk

You make me feel all sparkly
and shimmery inside.
Like a snow-globe that's been
turned upside down.

Yellow roses! YELLOW ROSES?!
How did you know? x

You're my absolute favourite mistake ;) x

This morning I didn't even want to smile. By lunchtime you had me laughing. Bring on dinner!

I love it because you never give me mixed signals. I always know where I am with you.

You had me @ 'hello'.

It's the weekend, the sun is shining and I'm seeing you. What more could a guy want?

As one-night-stands go that was pretty life changing! x

All of a sudden I, Miss Independent Woman, don't want my own space. I want to share it with you.

Einstein was right. I put my hand in a flame for a second and it feels like an hour. But one hour with you is like a minute.

People keep asking me

'Why the big smile?'

Hmm, wonder why?!

You read Men are from
Mars and didn't make me
read it. You get it and I
love you for that. x

You have my heart and my soul in the palm of your hand. You just don't know it yet.

You. Me.
Mailroom. Now.
That is all.

When my head says
'Who cares?'
my heart shouts
'You do!'

Every
memory
before
you
is
meaningless.

#iloveyoubecause...

...you always get it, and I don't have to explain.

...you don't try to be perfect. Or mind because I'm not.

...you make me think about things I've never thought about before.

...you love me for what I am, not what I've got.

...you keep it real and you don't play games with me. Except Mousetrap.

...you're always yourself. You don't turn into some uptight pseudo-intellectual with other people.

...you're bonkers. Like me. So you make me feel normal.

...you didn't laugh at me when I cried in Toy Story 3.

...you don't make me worry about you looking at someone else.

...you didn't freak out when the puppy peed on your new shoes.

Today, I hit 500 followers
on Twitter and I want them
all to know: I love you!

I love that we were kicked off
speed dating for not moving
when the bell went. x

I'm praying for a snow storm
tonight, so we can get snowed in
together...even though it's July.

Je ne regrette rien.
Especially not you.

You are the best diet I've
ever been on. I think of
you instead of food.
All the time.

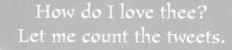

How do I love thee?
Let me count the tweets.

I've just changed my status from
'single' to 'in a relationship'.
No going back now!

My life is like a fairytale. Once upon a time there was me, then there was my handsome prince, and now it's happily ever after.

I love you for buying me the
Take That album even though
you can't stand them.

You make me feel like a star, even
though I'm just an ordinary girl
from Preston with a mousy bob
and knobbly knees.

I've always had two left feet, but with you I can dance till dawn.
Salsa till sunset. Tango till...teatime?

Hey – who gets the tap end
tonight then?

I used to want stuff –
clothes, handbags, shoes
– now all I want is you.

You make me feel like a bottle of champagne after a Grand Prix win.

I'm not bothered about Tiffany – the ring off a Coke can would be just fine...

Nietzsche said there is always some madness in love. I'm so glad I have an excuse for my virtual insanity.

I'm so glad I met you. I was getting tired of kissing frogs ;)

Love
hurts?

What.
Ever.
xxx

You're the missing part of my jigsaw. It took me ages to find you because you haven't got a straight edge.

Life with you is just going way too fast...

I know I talk rubbish half the time, but I love it because you listen.

When you really love someone, age is just a number.

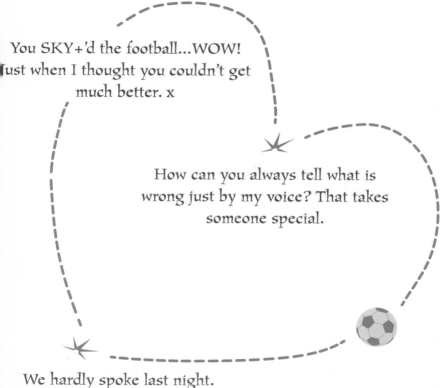

You SKY+'d the football...WOW! Just when I thought you couldn't get much better. x

How can you always tell what is wrong just by my voice? That takes someone special.

We hardly spoke last night. We didn't need to. I like that. xxx

I'm going to be thrown out of my bookclub tonight because I haven't read the book. I've been spending too much time with you!

Carlsberg don't
make girlfriends,
but if they did...

I love the me I am when I am
with you. I like her so much
better than the other me.

You are the only person who
could make me forget the
Jimmy Choo sample sale.

In answer to your question,
if you can tell me my favourite
ice cream, then the answer is YES
crosses fingers

If **love is blind**, why am I shopping in Agent Provocateur?

At least when you're away
and I look out at the night
sky, I know we're looking at
the same moon.

I gotta feeling, that
today's gonna be a good
day, a good good day...
I'm seeing you! xxx

Does this have to be either
love or lust?
Can't it be both? :)

I'd rather have beans
on toast with you than a
Michelin star meal with
George Clooney. Fact.

You looked gorgeous this morning.
I am a very lucky man.

When I'm running low on
inspiration, I think of you and it
fires me up again. x

Love is...not worrying about making
a fool of yourself on Twitter.
I love you.

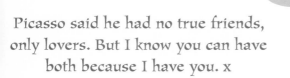

Picasso said he had no true friends,
only lovers. But I know you can have
both because I have you. x

I love you. A second to say but a lifetime to prove. I've got my whole life ahead of me.

I know it's the real thing because you're going to meet my family this weekend and I DON'T CARE WHAT THEY THINK!

I love it when you slide your arms
around me when I'm doing the
washing up. (But I'd love it even
more if you did the washing up...!)

OH MY GOD!

You made me slow dance. To
George Michael Careless Whisper!
My cred is so blown,

but I don't care!

You stole my taxi. And
then you stole my heart.
You sir, are a thief.

There's only one thing
I'd change about you...
your surname.

I found my first grey hair today.
But I don't care because I know you
won't see it...will you?! xx

I took a gamble when I fell in love
with you, but the odds were better
than the 3.20 at Cheltenham.
Looks like I backed a winner.

Just in case you're checking Twitter
for the hundredth time: I got stuck
in a tunnel with no signal.
No? Just me then!

Two peas in a pod? Hardly, but who cares? You're awesome.

I know we've only been together a short while (and I'm too shy to say this out loud) but I, umm, really like you... like really like you.

My life began at 41
and three quarters.

The day I met you.

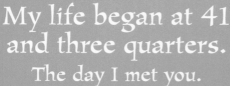

For you I would give up The X Factor,
gum and cupcakes. And for those who
know me, that's saying something.

Just saw an old pic of us
on facebook. You really
are gorgeous! xx

You're the man of my dreams.
But I always forget my
dreams when I wake up.
Fancy reminding me? xx

If love is blind,
guess I should have
gone to Specsavers.

Your tweets leave my heart
all a-twitter! xox

You're one in a million.
In a good way.

Just because I haven't tweeted you
doesn't mean I don't love you...
I'm just waiting for you to
tweet me!

I love you because you're
there when I need you. But I
love you even more because
you're there when I don't!

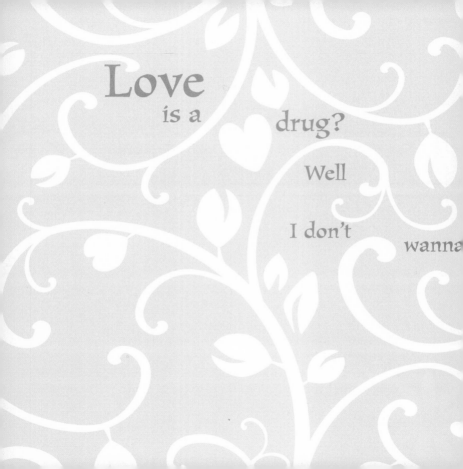

go   to   rehab.   Ever.

No

no

no.

There's a part of me missing when you're not there. My wallet ...joke. XOX

Thinking of you wastes so much of my time.

I'm going to get fired! xxx

My trainer thinks I've been seeing another trainer. Don't want to admit how I've been burning the calories...!

T'is better to have loved and lost than to have never loved at all.(@Tennyson)

Thank you for always tweeting me like a princess :)

Only from the heart can you touch the sky. (@JalaluddinRumi)

I put the bins out this morning. Just for you. xxx

When you walked into my life, I realised
why it hadn't worked with anyone else
before. Thank you. xoxo

My last boyfriend had
a porsche, but I much
prefer going on the
Tube with you.

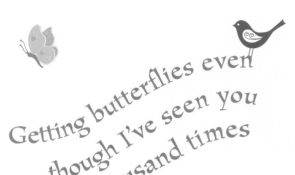

Getting butterflies even
though I've seen you
a thousand times

xox

Love is the irresistible desire to be irresistibly desired. (@MarkTwain)

We've known each other for a long time now. And I've always been one to beat around the bush instead of...What I'm trying to say is I love y

I'm the luckiest man in the world.
You're all mine.

Forget the party, I want to
spend the night looking
after you. Just don't give
me the lurgy... xxx

If we were in the Big Brother house, the audience would see it coming a mile off. xxx

That giant pink panther you bought me for when you're not here? He's just not as cuddly.

Spotted! Hot girl on the 185 bus today, reading Catch-22, wearing a red beret. I can't get you out of my mind.

I love you more than I love beer. And pizza. Combined.

Hey, we HAVE to go to the supermarket. Sorry.

But I'll make it up to you. Promise ;) xx

I'd rather have a
nanosecond with you than
an eternity without.

It's impossible for me to stop
loving you – my mind says
'Move on' but my heart won't
let you go.

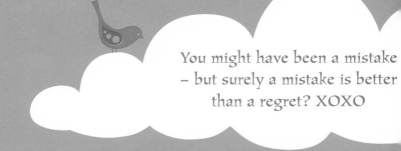

You might have been a mistake – but surely a mistake is better than a regret? XOXO

You crack me up. Your jokes are terrible, I mean, really bad. But you still make me laugh xxxx

I'm wearing your cardigan.
Does that mean it must be a
boyfriend cardigan?! xx

Our song just came on the radio.
Thinking of you.

I can't believe you've noticed me too.
These things never happen to me. Yay!

Hey cupcake,
did I tell you
I love you?

Thank you for turning this
ugly bug into a butterfly.

I know it's love.

You used every pan I own to make
that green curry and

I don't even care!

I know your kind. I know I shouldn't but
I just can't resist. I'm done for! x

You bring out the
best in me.
Love. xxx

Who'd have thought it? After twelve years of chemistry, I finally pluck up the courage and you say 'yes'. Whoopee!

I woke up to a tweet from you...love it :)

I can't sleep. For the first time, reality is better than my dreams. xoxo

You know that birthmark on your knee that you hate? Well I even love that ;) x

I'm not with you because I think I can live with you, but because I know I can't live without you.

A kiss makes the heart young again and wipes out the years.
(@RupertBrooke)

How did you know that the way to my heart is through my stomach? Raspberry crème brûlée and I was done for.

Whenever I hear that woman on the tube say 'Mind the gap', I think of us and say 'Who cares?'

I want to run across the beach into
your arms. Bleurgh, corny, I know
but that's what you do to me!

I know I love you because I miss
you and you haven't even gone
yet...I can still hear you in the
shower. You can't sing!

Only our second take-away and you remembered the prawn toast? It must be love!

I really thought I'd got the measure of
you. But then you went and did that.
Don't stop surprising me! x

Your side of the bed is
still warm. I'm missing
you already.

Every time I
being on the

, my tummy drops like
k of a bus going over a hill.

When I said I was freezing in bed this morning?
Yeah, I was lying. xxx

Love is composed of a single soul
inhabiting two bodies. (@Aristotle)

Don't let the lads see, but I'm going to skip the
footie tonight to be with you.

Tell me you're free?

I went through about 20
aftershaves in the shop today
trying to find the one you wear.
Consider yourself stalked. x

It's funny how you never believe
in The One, until they come
along. Yours smugly. x